Gangs and Your Neighborhood

TOOKIE SPEAKS OUT AGAINST GANG VIOLENCE™

Stanley "Tookie" Williams

with Barbara Cottman Becnel

The Rosen Publishing Group's
PowerKids Press™
New York

Published in 1996 by The Rosen Publishing Group, Inc.
29 East 21st Street, New York, NY 10010

First Edition

Book design: Kim Sonsky

Photo credits: Cover © Mimi Cotter/International Stock; front cover inset, back cover and p. 4 © J. Patrick Forden; p. 7 © Bill Stanton/International Stock; p. 8 © Lisa Terry/Impact Visuals; p. 11 by John Novajosky; p. 12 © Ron Sachs/Archive Photos; p. 15 © Roger Markham Smith/International Stock; p. 16 © Judy Gurovitz/International Stock; p. 19 by Seth Dinnerman; p. 20 © Joe Willis/International Stock.

Williams, Stanley.
    Gangs and your neighborhood/ by Stanley "Tookie" Williams and Barbara Cottman Becnel.
       p.   cm. — (Tookie speaks out against gang violence)
    Includes index.
    Summary: Argues against joining gangs because such groups hurt people and neighborhoods.
    ISBN 0-8239-2347-9
    1. Gangs—United States—Juvenile literature. 2. Juvenile delinquency—United States—Juvenile literature. 3. Neighborhood—United States—Juvenile literature. [1. Gangs. 2. Neighborhood.] I. Becnel, Barbara Cottman. II. Title. III. Series: Williams, Stanley. Tookie speaks out against gang violence.
HV6439.U5W576 1996
364.1'06'60973—dc20
                                                95-51329
                                                CIP
                                                  AC

Manufactured in the United States of America

Contents

My New Neighborhood

I was almost seven when my mother and I left Shreveport, Louisiana, and moved to South Central Los Angeles. Mother moved us hoping that life in this new city would be better for me, her only son.

Our first apartment in South Central was small, neat, and clean. The grass in our yard was bright green and very pretty. Anyone driving around my neighborhood would have thought that I lived in a really nice part of town. But I learned that living in South Central wasn't as good as it looked.

◀ *Tookie's neighborhood in South Central looked pretty but was made dangerous by gang violence.*

Life in the 'Hood

I saw a lot of violence and crime in South Central. I saw so many bad things that I stopped caring about what was right and wrong. I accepted the way things were in my new **'hood** (HOOD), or neighborhood.

My friends stole from other people to get the clothes and food their parents couldn't afford to buy them. I wanted to fit in with them, so I was willing to do anything they did. That was a big mistake. Violence and crime became part of my everyday life.

Many people are hurt by violence and crime. ▶

The New Gang in Town

By the time I was 17, there were many gangs in South Central. My friends and I were always getting into fights with them. So when Raymond Washington asked me to join forces with him and his friends to protect our 'hood from harm, I said okay. Soon after, we started a gang called the Crips.

We thought that no one else could help us take care of the 'hood. Everyone was too scared. So we looked out for ourselves. But we ended up hurting our 'hood more than helping it.

◀ *Gang members sometimes risk their lives for their neighborhoods.*

9

Fighting for Our 'Hood

Soon the Crips were no longer fighting just to protect the people in our 'hood. We had started fighting for the 'hood itself.

By then we believed that the 'hood belonged to us. We began to think it was okay to hurt others just for walking through our 'hood. We thought that hurting others, or being hurt for our 'hood, was a good thing. We were wrong.

South Central became an even more dangerous place to live because of the Crips and other gangs.

Gang members usually end up hurting neighborhoods more than helping them. ▶

Street Soldiers

Many gang members call themselves street soldiers. We did. A **street soldier** (STREET SOL-jer) is a person willing to fight for, and even die for, his gang.

Being a street soldier is a crazy way to live. And it's not being a true soldier. A true soldier joins an army to help protect his people and his homeland from being hurt. A street soldier usually joins a gang to prove he is tough. A street soldier sometimes fights to protect his people or his 'hood. But usually he fights to impress his friends.

◀ *True soldiers, such as Colin Powell, fight to protect their country, not to prove how tough they are.*

Gangbanging Hurts Everyone

We started out as street soldiers fighting for our 'hood. But before long we were using violence to rob stores, steal cars, and sell drugs. That's called **gangbanging** (GANG-bang-ing).

When kids gangbang, innocent people get hurt. Sometimes kids even younger than you are shot or killed. It's not fair, and it's not right. But that's what happens when people gangbang. Gangbanging hurts everyone in the 'hood.

Sometimes innocent people die as a result of gangbanging and gang violence. ▶

It's Okay to Care

Your 'hood is where your family, friends, and home are. It's where you spend a lot of time. So it's okay to want to take care of your 'hood. But it's not okay to hurt or to kill people, sell drugs, or commit other crimes. These things don't help your 'hood.

If you really care about your 'hood, you won't put your family and friends in danger. If you really care about your 'hood, you'll want to do good things to make it a safe place to be.

◄ *One way to make your neighborhood a fun place to be is to play sports together.*

You Are Your Neighborhood

You and all the other people in your neighborhood make your 'hood whatever it is—good or bad. It's up to you and those who live there to make your 'hood a nice place to live.

Be smart about who you hang out with. If you're not a gang member, don't become one. If you are a gang member, don't gang-bang or do other violent things. Be by yourself if that's what it takes to break away from gangbanging. That's how you can take good care of yourself—and your 'hood.

Glossary

gangbanging (GANG-bang-ing) When gang members hurt other people or commit crimes.

'hood (HOOD) Slang word for neighborhood.

street soldier (STREET SOL-jer) Gang member who is willing to fight or die for his gang.

Index

DISCARDED